GARBAGE and RECYCLING

BY JUDITH WOODBURN

ENVIRONMENT ALERT!

Gareth Stevens Publishing
MILWAUKEE

For a free color catalog describing Gareth Stevens' list of high-quality books, call
1-800-341-3569 (USA) or 1-800-461-9120 (Canada).

Library of Congress Cataloging-in-Publication Data

Woodburn, Judith, 1959-
    Garbage and recycling / Judith Woodburn.
        p.   cm. — (Environment alert!)
    Includes bibliographical references and index.
    Summary: Discusses the solid waste crisis, the cause of landfill crowding, and solutions in
recycling various substances.
    ISBN 0-8368-0700-6
    1. Refuse and refuse disposal—Juvenile literature. 2. Recycling (Waste, etc.)—Juvenile
literature. [1. Refuse and refuse disposal. 2. Recycling (Waste)] I. Title. II. Series.
TD792.W66 1991
363.72'85—dc20   91-50343

Edited, designed, and produced by
Gareth Stevens Publishing
1555 North RiverCenter Drive, Suite 201
Milwaukee, WI 53212, USA

Picture Credits:

© Bryan and Cherry Alexander, p. 9 (upper); Courtesy of Aluminum Company of
America, p. 20; © Lyn Alweis/The Denver Post, p. 26 (upper and lower); © Erwin and
Peggy Bauer/Bruce Coleman Limited, front cover (inset), title; © Charles Bowman/
Picture Perfect USA, p. 27; © Verna Brainard/PHOTRI, p. 11; Sharone Burris, 1991,
p. 13, p. 25 (right); © Dennis Capolongo/Greenpeace, p. 12, pp. 12-13; Kurt
Carloni/Artisan, 1992, pp. 6-7; © Peter Clarke/Survival Anglia, p. 14 (right); ©
Gerald Cubitt/Bruce Coleman Limited, p. 5; © John D. Cunningham/Visuals
Unlimited, p. 18 (upper); © Mark Edwards/Still Pictures, p. 18 (lower); © Greg Evans
International, p. 14 (left); © Michael Freeman/Bruce Coleman Limited, p. 9 (lower);
© Arthur R. Hill/Visuals Unlimited, p. 16; Rick Karpinski/DeWalt & Associates,
1992, p. 7, pp. 10-11, p. 21 (upper); © William E. Larose/Greenpeace, pp. 2-3; ©
Brian North/Picture Perfect USA, p. 23 (upper); © Photo Network, pp. 24-25, p. 25
(left); © Picture Perfect USA, p. 23 (lower); © Roger Scruton/IMPACT Photos, p.
17; © Simon Shepheard/IMPACT Photos, cover; Tim Spransy, 1991, pp. 28-29; ©
Gareth Stevens, Inc., 1992, p. 22; © TROPIX/M & V Birley, p. 4, p. 8; © Alex
Williams/Greenpeace, p. 21 (lower); © David Woodfall/NHPA, pp. 22-23; Courtesy
of Woodland Park Zoo, p. 19; © Peter Ziminski/Visuals Unlimited, p. 15.

Series editor: Patricia Lantier-Sampon
Series designer: Laurie Shock
Book designer: Sabine Beaupré
Picture researcher: Diane Laska
Research editor: David Kent

Printed in the United States of America

  2 3 4 5 6 7 8 9 97 96 95 94 93

At this time, Gareth Stevens, Inc., does not use 100 percent recycled paper, although
the paper used in our books does contain about 30 percent recycled fiber. This
decision was made after a careful study of current recycling procedures revealed their
dubious environmental benefits. We will continue to explore recycling options.

Gareth Stevens
President

CONTENTS

Words that appear in the glossary are printed in **boldface** type the first time they appear in the text.

Too much trash

We don't usually stop to think about it, but every time we unwrap a stick of gum, use a paper towel, or finish a can of soda, we are contributing to one of the world's biggest **pollution** problems: trash. Each person in the United States produces an average of half a ton of garbage every year! What happens to all this trash when we are done with it? A tiny amount is saved and used again. Some is burned. Most, however, goes into huge piles of trash called **landfills**. Some landfills can get as tall as a skyscraper.

Above: The world's garbage problem begins with individual people who don't take responsibility for their trash.

Every year, wealthy countries like the United States, Canada, and France make more and more trash. And there is less and less room for it. Our landfills are filling up, making ugly mountains of garbage everywhere from Switzerland to Singapore.

Trash is not only ugly; it's dangerous and wasteful, too. Burning it creates air pollution. Burying it can cause poisons from the trash to leak into streams and rivers, creating water pollution. We need to develop better ways of handling trash. Otherwise, our world will just become more and more polluted, harming animals and endangering our health.

Opposite: A crowded landfill in Bombay, India.

5

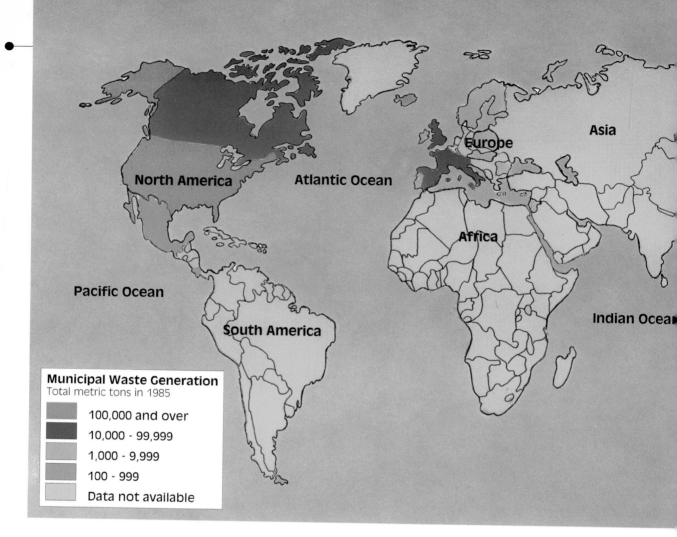

Municipal Waste Generation
Total metric tons in 1985

- 100,000 and over
- 10,000 - 99,999
- 1,000 - 9,999
- 100 - 999
- Data not available

Asia

Europe

North America

Atlantic Ocean

Africa

Pacific Ocean

South America

Indian Ocean

The Trash-makers

Trash is everywhere. Some countries, however, are bigger trash-makers than others. The United States is the worst trash-maker in the world. Because the U.S. population is larger and because Americans use far more disposable products and products with wasteful packaging, Americans end up throwing away more trash than people in nearly every other industrialized country and nine times as much trash as people in poorer countries in Africa or Central America.

Above: This map of the world shows the estimated amount of garbage produced by the people of different countries on a yearly basis. Richer countries tend to produce more trash because the people there can afford to consume more products, which then must be thrown away.

Australia

Right: Disposable straws, napkins, cups, and other such products are signs of our throwaway culture.

Our Throwaway Habits

Years ago, our grandparents and great-grandparents didn't make so much trash. It was harder to get products in the first place, and they didn't come with so much packaging. What people did buy was used and reused. Old clothes were made into cleaning rags or cut up to make patches for beautiful patchwork quilts. People saved the collars and cuffs from old shirts to put on new shirts. During World War II, children collected bottles and cans and sold them for spare change.

Today, almost everything is disposable. We throw away cups, napkins, toys, even cameras. In the United States, 1.6 billion pens go into the garbage each year! Our food comes wrapped in costly packages that we throw away after a few minutes.

It doesn't make much sense to pay for things we're just going to throw away, but this habit seems to be getting worse. Companies that sell products think no one will buy them unless they have lots of fancy packaging.

Above: In a health food store in England, shoppers can find food without a lot of unnecessary packaging.

Right: At a bazaar in Pakistan, spices are still sold in bulk. That is, they do not come in packages, and shoppers may buy as much — or as little — as they want.

Opposite: If you had lived when your grandparents were young, your old shirt or dress might have ended up in a pretty patchwork quilt.

Why Landfills Don't Work

Not long ago, we used to call landfills dumps. People drove to the dump and tossed garbage into an open pit. But problems occurred as more and more people used the dumps. The dumps attracted rats and bugs. Rain filtered through the garbage, washing out **toxic** substances into nearby land and water supplies. Something had to be done.

So dumps began to change. Soon they were called landfills, and each day the garbage was bulldozed over with dirt and sprayed with disinfectant to keep rodents away.

Below: This landfill illustrates how most cities take care of their collective garbage. Garbage trucks carry the refuse to a dumping area, where the garbage is released into a large hole lined with plastic. Each portion of the landfill is carefully constructed to contain a certain amount of garbage and is set off by a pipe framework. As layers of garbage are added to the landfill, new plastic liners and soil are periodically placed on top, with bulldozers moving the soil into the appropriate areas. This system is the most effective method of taking care of garbage to date.

But even though this was an improvement, there was still one more problem. The landfills began filling up. One reason this happens is that air and sunlight can't get to the items in landfills because so much garbage and dirt is piled up. Since most materials need air and light to **decompose**, they just sit in the landfill, taking up space. One scientist dug up a 10-year-old newspaper in a landfill — and it was still easy to read!

When landfills fill up, people usually do not want to open new ones. The land required for landfills is expensive, and the garbage is ugly. Often, people want to use the space for better things, like parks or homes.

Recycling a Landfill

When the city dump in Virginia Beach, VA, began filling up more than twenty years ago, city leaders decided to turn it into something beautiful. So they covered the landfill with soil and built a park with tennis courts, playgrounds, and skate ramps. In one part of the park, they began piling up new trash to make a mountain. City planners thought it would take about twenty years to get enough trash, but people made so much garbage that the mountain was done in 4.5 years. The people of the city named it Mt. Trashmore and covered it with soil and grass. But about six years ago, Mt. Trashmore began leaking. Water from rain built up in the layers of garbage and leaked out the side of the hill, creating dirty pools of contaminated water. Virginia Beach's city leaders still have not been able to completely solve this unfortunate problem.

FACT FILE: Garbage with No Place to Go

Sometimes, no matter how much a community is willing to pay, it may not be able to find anyone to take its garbage. This happened in 1987, when the Mobro garbage **barge** carried more than 3,000 tons of garbage away from Long Island in New York.

For months, the Mobro barge sailed to three states and four different countries, but no one would take the garbage. People did not want to fill up their landfills with someone else's trash.

So the smelly barge of trash returned to New York, and it sat in the harbor while flies buzzed around it. An environmental group hung a sign on the barge that read: "Next Time, Try **Recycling**." Eventually the garbage on the Mobro barge was incinerated, leaving 400 tons of ashes, which still had to be buried in a landfill.

Above and opposite: The Mobro garbage barge back at anchor near New York.

Right: The route of the Mobro garbage barge as it went in search of a home for its smelly cargo.

United States

Gulf of Mexico

Mexico

Cuba

Belize

Caribbean Sea

How Trash Hurts Sea Animals

More than 14 billion pounds (6.4 billion kg) of trash per year are carelessly thrown into the oceans of the world. One of the biggest problems for sea animals is plastic trash, because plastic trash never breaks down, or decomposes. Most of the trash that floats on the surface of the ocean is plastic.

Above: A gannet's bill has been roped by a carelessly disposed-of nylon cord.

Left: Garbage is not just ugly to look at. A littered beach like this one can be dangerous to the many animals who live and hunt for food near it and the people who walk along the water's edge.

Seabirds eat little pieces of plastic on the beaches because they look like food. The plastic fills the birds' stomachs so they cannot eat real food, and they starve. Turtles eat plastic bags thinking they are their favorite food — jellyfish — and they die.

Above: In the summer of 1990, Americans discovered a new and frightening source of litter. Some hospitals were not disposing of their garbage properly, so needles and other used medical products were washing up on beaches where people swam.

Plastic six-pack rings do more than just keep soda cans together. If people throw them away without cutting the rings apart first, they can act like nooses. The rings get around animals' necks, choking them as they grow. It is sad to see animals die simply because someone could not take the trouble to dispose of his or her trash properly.

TAMING THE TRASH MONSTER

Incineration: Trash Goes Up in Smoke

Incineration, or burning, is one way communities try to get rid of their garbage. The garbage is dumped into large incinerators and burned at very high temperatures. A small amount of residue, or **ash,** is left.

Some people think incinerators are a great idea because they seem to get rid of lots of trash quickly. And in some countries, such as Denmark, garbage is burned to create energy.

But incineration creates problems, too. It sends toxic fumes into the air, and dangerous materials, such as batteries and other poisonous garbage, are not always removed from the garbage before it is burned. As a result, the leftover ash is often poisonous. Because the ash is toxic, it is hard to dispose of safely.

Above: Garbage incinerators like this one burn trash at temperatures over 1800°F (982°C), creating harmless steam along with dangerous pollution.

Opposite: Because incinerators create huge amounts of air pollution, they are often placed on ships that can sail far from populated areas.

16

17

Composting: Turning Trash Back into Nature

Composting is an old-fashioned way of taking care of trash. People in many countries take their **organic** trash, such as vegetable scraps and coffee grounds, to their gardens and toss it onto what they call the "compost heap." Slowly, tiny **bacteria**, oxygen, and moisture work on the trash, turning it into sweet-smelling, useful compost. This **humus**-like compost is rich in nutrients and, when used as fertilizer, helps plants grow better.

Above: A compost heap can be used as a dumping area for much of our daily garbage. This growing pile of refuse should be moved around in the soil with a shovel every now and then so that the garbage can decompose more quickly.

Left: Schoolchildren add materials to a compost heap. In a few months, the materials in the pile will break down. Then they can be safely returned to the earth. This simple process could reduce by half the volume of trash now being carted to landfills.

Over time, many people forgot about composting. It seemed easier just to throw things away. But now, many people are starting to compost their trash again. Companies are finding ways to compost their trash, too.

Some people have gotten very good at composting. Sweden composts one-fourth of its **solid waste**. In Seattle, Washington, the manure from elephants at the zoo is composted and given away free to gardeners as fertilizer. They call it "Zoo Doo."

Below: Elephants produce tons of manure every week. They don't know it, but their wastes are helping flowers bloom all over Seattle!

Recycling: Finding Treasures in Trash

Recycling is a fancy word for a simple idea: making trash into something usable instead of just throwing it out. Most of what's in our trash can be recycled. Glass can be melted and made into new bottles over and over again. **Aluminum** cans can be melted down and made into new cans. Paper can be washed, ground up, and made into new paper. Many plastic items, such as milk and soda bottles, can be melted into new, useful forms, like plastic flower pots.

To recycle, we separate the useful things, such as newspapers, bottles, and cans, from the rest of our garbage. Many communities have recycling centers that will pay for these materials to sell to companies that want to use them to make something new.

Some countries are doing a great job of recycling: Japan and the Netherlands recycle more than half of their aluminum, paper, and glass. But in the United States, only 13 percent of all the garbage is recycled. Hopefully, as more companies start buying the recycled materials, more people will recycle, too.

Many children and adults now make a special effort to collect their aluminum cans instead of dumping them in the trash. This way, the cans can be taken to a recycling center, where they are weighed. The collectors receive a small amount of money in return for their recycling efforts.

Left: The average garbage can holds many items that could be recycled instead of being thrown away. Most recycling centers will accept glass bottles and jars, plastic milk and soda containers, aluminum cans, and newspapers.

Below: Many communities now have two types of trash collection trucks — one for garbage and one for recyclable materials.

Precycling: Unmaking Trash

No matter how good we get at recycling, it solves only part of the garbage problem. After all, not all trash can be recycled, and the recycling process uses valuable energy.

The best way to keep ourselves from drowning in trash is not to create trash in the first place. This is called *precycling*.

Cutting Back on Fast-Food Garbage

Fast-food companies create a lot of trash. Since everything they sell is wrapped individually, they use lots of packaging. Some companies, however, are trying to change. In 1991, McDonald's promised to reduce its production of trash by 80 percent! This includes making paper napkins a bit smaller, eliminating foam containers and single-serving ketchup packets, and replacing paper cups with reusable mugs. By themselves, these steps don't seem like much, but when you're trying to cut back on trash, every little bit counts.

Right: Cloth bags and wicker baskets are all reusable containers for groceries.

It's not that hard to understand precycling. Instead of using disposable materials, use reusable things. Using cloth diapers instead of paper ones and reusable pens instead of disposable ones is precycling. Another way is to use a cloth or string shopping bag to carry groceries home, as many people in Europe do, instead of paper or plastic bags.

Disposable diapers (left) create 6.5 million tons of garbage every year. A cloth diaper (above) can be reused again and again, creating far less waste.

FACT FILE: The Art of Recycling

In Watts, a poor neighborhood of Los Angeles, California, a man named Simon Rodia spent 33 years making enormous towers out of junk nobody wanted. Old pipes, bedsprings, and broken dishes — all went into his huge sculptures. By the time he was done, one of Simon Rodia's sculptures was more than 60 feet (18 m) tall!

Below and opposite: Simon Rodia's huge scrap sculptures attract visitors from all over the world.

Machida, Japan: A City That Recycles

The 340,000 people living in Machida, Japan, create more than 100,000 tons of garbage a year. But they can't just throw it away. There's no room for landfills in the tiny country of Japan! Instead, all of Machida's garbage goes to a beautiful waste recycling center. The people of Machida are proud of their recycling center.

Inside the center, big magnets separate recyclable steel from the rest of the garbage. Computer-controlled machines handle most of the work. But the machines wouldn't work very well if the people of Machida didn't do their part by carefully separating cans, bottles, paper, and plastic before throwing things out.

The system has a big impact. As one magazine reported, if all of Machida's garbage for a year were recycled into paper, it could make a roll of toilet paper that would wrap around the Earth ten times!

25

Garbage Is Our Newest Resource

There is so much trash in the world that our garbage problem sometimes seems overwhelming. Unlike some forms of pollution that often sneak unseen into our air and water, we see garbage everywhere — floating on the ocean and littering our streets and sidewalks. But because we can see it, garbage may be the easiest pollution problem to solve. It's easier to clean up than pollution that has mixed with the soil, air, or water.

It really pays to reduce our garbage. Products that aren't heavily packaged are usually cheaper. And all over the world, people and companies are learning that there is treasure in trash. Some companies are paving streets with ground-up old tires. Other people are learning to build homes from recycled materials — including cans and bottles.

There are countless ways to make better use of our trash. If each of us learns to see garbage as a resource, not refuse, we can keep our planet clean and beautiful.

Above: In Denver, Colorado, people are experimenting with aluminum cans to build houses. They're not pretty, but the cans have advantages: they are inexpensive and lightweight, and they keep a house warm by trapping air inside the walls.

Opposite: By precycling and recycling, we can keep our cities clear of trash. Beautiful cities, such as Singapore, will remain wonderful, healthy places to live.

27

RESEARCH ACTIVITIES

1. Find out how much trash you make. For a week, take every bit of trash you make — gum wrappers, papers, soda cans, fruit peels, even the food left on your plate — and keep it in a separate bag. At the end of the week, weigh the bag (or bags). How much waste did you make? How much waste would you make in a year? How much of the trash was something you didn't need to use or could have used again instead of throwing away?

2. Visit your local landfill. With an adult, see if you can arrange a visit to the landfill where your community's trash is disposed of. How big is it? Do you think you would want to have more landfills near your home or school? What kinds of trash do you see at the landfill? Could some of what you see have been reused or recycled?

3. With your classmates, organize a clean-up day. You might decide to clean up a park, a beach, or a vacant lot. When the day comes, wear old clothes and gloves for picking up the really messy stuff. Take a photograph of what the area looks like before you clean it up, and when you're done, take another picture. How much of a difference did you and your classmates make?

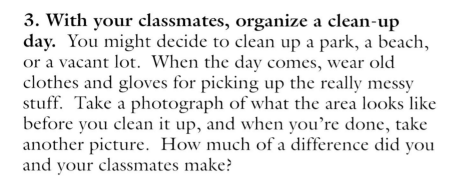

4. Make a recycled toy. Plastic squeeze bottles make great squirt guns. You can string together buttons to make necklaces or bracelets, and ice cream sticks are perfect "logs" to glue together for building. When you start thinking about it, you'll come up with many more ideas for recycled toys.

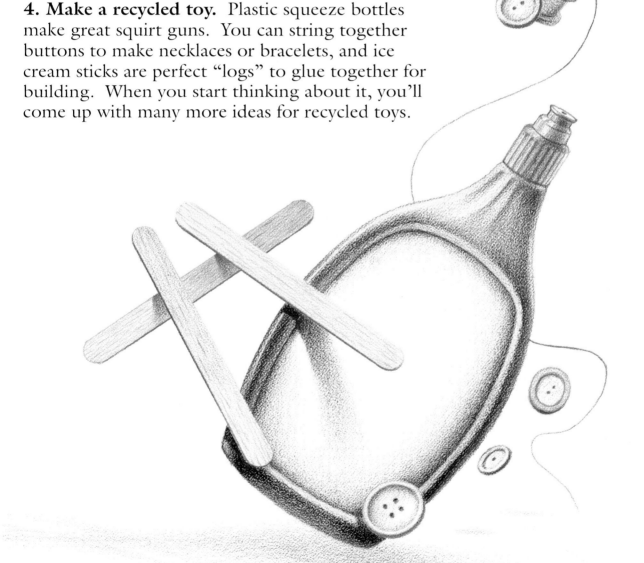

Things You Can Do to Help

1. **Find ways to cut back on waste yourself.** Write on both sides of paper and buy things that can be reused instead of thrown away. When shopping, ask for foods that don't come with a lot of extra packaging. Or, if you see a product that has too much wasteful packaging, write the company that manufactures the product and ask the people there to stop being wasteful.

2. **If you drink soda or other canned beverages, cut the six-pack rings before throwing them away.** Cut the tiny holes as well as the big ones.

3. **What you don't reuse, recycle.** Most cities have recycling centers, and once you get in the habit, it's easy to separate your plastic bottles, aluminum cans, paper, and glass from the rest of your garbage.

4. **Start a recycling program at your school if you don't have one already.** Each classroom can have special bins for recycling paper. In the lunchroom, you can separate cans and plastic from cups and utensils for recycling. Better yet, persuade your cafeteria to use reusable utensils, plates, and cups.

Places to Write for More Information

Greenpeace (Canada)
2623 West 4th Avenue
Vancouver, British
    Columbia V6K 1P8

The National Recycling
    Coalition
1101 30th Street NW,
    Suite 305
Washington, D.C. 20007

Center for Environmental
    Education
1725 DeSales Street NW
Washington, D.C. 20036

More Books to Read

Garbage, by Karen O'Connor (Lucent Books)
Save the Earth, by Betty Miles (Knopf)
Recyclopedia: Games, Science Equipment and Crafts from Recycled Materials,
    by Robin Simons (Boston Children's Museum, Houghton Mifflin)
50 Simple Things Kids Can Do to Save the Earth, by the Earthworks Group
    (Andrews and McNeel)

Glossary

aluminum — a silvery white metal used in making beverage cans and many other products.

ash — a soft, powdery residue left over from burning material.

bacteria — microscopic organisms. Bacteria in the soil help break down dead plants into humus, returning them to the soil.

barge — a long, flat-bottomed boat.

composting — the process by which organic wastes are allowed to decay and turn into humus-like material.

decompose — to break down a material into basic elements.

humus — a brown or black substance made up of decayed organic material. Humus adds nutrients to the soil and makes it easier for soil to hold water.

incineration — burning garbage until it is nothing but ashes.

landfills — special places where trash is dumped. Landfills are usually lined with clay or plastic, and each day's garbage is covered over with a thin layer of soil.

organic — anything made up of animal or vegetable matter. Organic materials in our garbage include fruit and vegetable peelings, meat scraps, and bones.

pollution — harmful waste materials in the air, soil, or water.

recycling — extracting useful materials from garbage and putting them through another "cycle" of use. When garbage is recycled, it is first sorted into categories of reusable materials, such as paper, glass, metal, and plastic.

solid waste — solid material that is thrown away, as opposed to sewage or other forms of liquid waste.

toxic — poisonous.

Index